GO TO THE POLLS

THE INSIDE SCOOP ON
VOTING AND ELECTIONS

WRITTEN BY JESSICA GUNDERSON

ILLUSTRATED BY LUIZ FERNANDO DA SILVA

CAPSTONE PRESS
a capstone imprint

Published by Capstone Press, an imprint of Capstone
1710 Roe Crest Drive, North Mankato, Minnesota 56003
capstonepub.com

Library of Congress Cataloging-in-Publication Data is available on the Library of Congress website.
ISBN: 9781669076193 (hardcover)
ISBN: 9781669076148 (paperback)
ISBN: 9781669076155 (ebook PDF)

Summary: Playful graphics and text take readers on a historical tour of the basis for the voting and election system in the United States, including lesser-known inside information.

Editorial Credits
Editor: Mandy Robbins; Designer: Heidi Thompson; Production Specialist: Tori Abraham

Printed and bound in the USA. 5853

CONTENTS

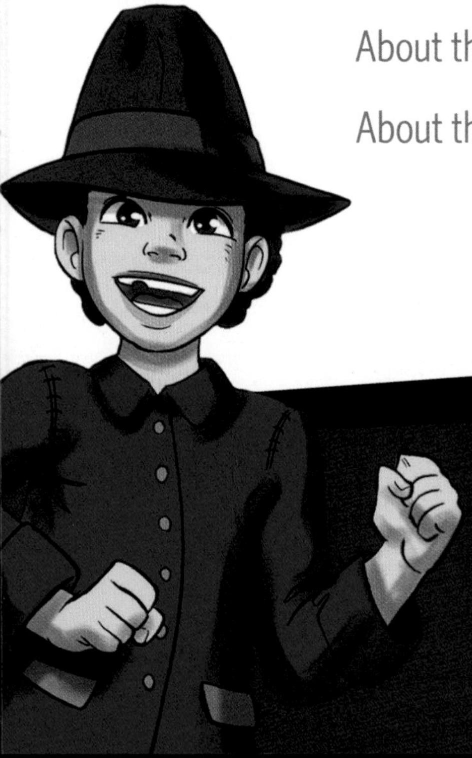

National elections, called general elections, are held every two years. Voters choose members of the United States Congress. Every four years, voters choose the U.S. president.

States have different ways to vote. Some use paper ballots. Others use voting machines.

Election winners are announced online, on the radio, in newspapers, and on television.

Who won?

We have to wait until the votes are counted to find out.

Elections determine government leaders. These people make laws for our country. People also vote on money for schools and other public projects. Voting helps shape our society.

You think voters in early America had a hard time voting? Today astronauts cast their ballots from space.

ALWAYS ON TUESDAYS

Elections in the U.S. are always on Tuesdays. In early America, people often had to travel to vote. Sundays were religious days. And Wednesdays were market days, when farmers sold their crops. Elections were held on Tuesdays so people could use Monday to travel, vote on Tuesday, and be back home by Wednesday.

CHAPTER ONE

VOTING IN HISTORY

Voting is necessary to American democracy. But voting existed long before the United States did.

Ancient Europe

Rome

Greece

The Greeks created the first democracy about 2,500 years ago. Every male citizen in ancient Greece over the age of 18 could vote in the Assembly. The Assembly was held 40 times a year on a hill in Athens.

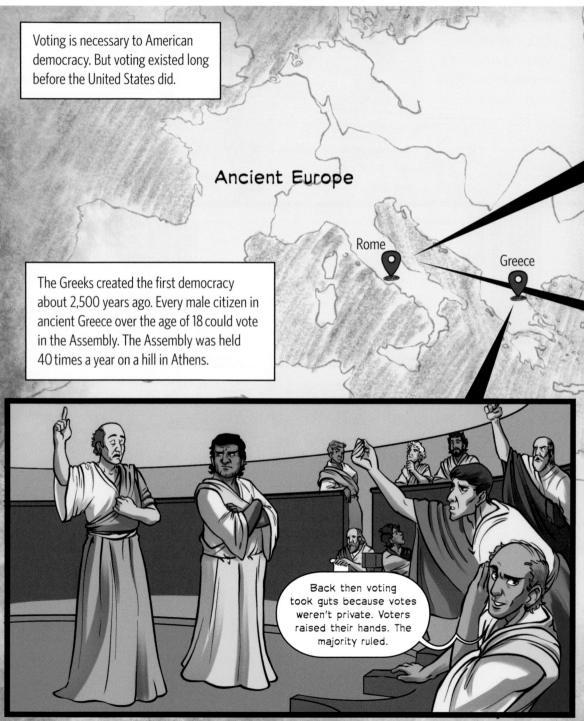

Back then voting took guts because votes weren't private. Voters raised their hands. The majority ruled.

In ancient Rome, adult male citizens voted publicly.

Pssst. Vote for me.

For one more coin.

Fine. I'll know if you don't.

Candidates often bribed voters with gifts or money.

Vote for me.

Nope. I'll vote how I want.

Eventually, voting became private. The United States would model its voting methods on those of ancient Greece and Rome.

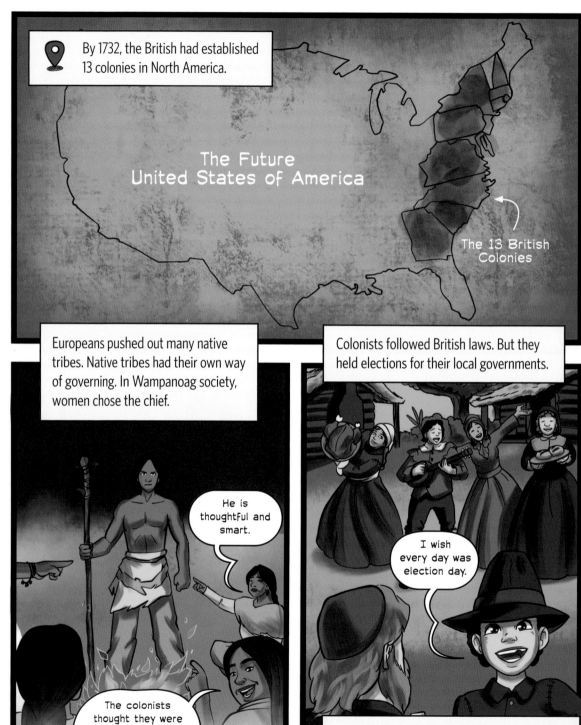

By 1732, the British had established 13 colonies in North America.

The Future
United States of America

The 13 British Colonies

Europeans pushed out many native tribes. Native tribes had their own way of governing. In Wampanoag society, women chose the chief.

He is thoughtful and smart.

The colonists thought they were more advanced than us, but our women could vote hundreds of years before theirs did.

Colonists followed British laws. But they held elections for their local governments.

I wish every day was election day.

Elections were festive. Colonists held parades and parties. Everyone ate and danced.

In most towns, only white male landowners could vote. Voting was done in public.

Your name and how you vote.

Sometimes colonists voted in groups.

All who vote "Yes," on that side. Everyone voting "No," on the other side.

Before George Washington became president, he served in the local Virginia government.

Vote for me.

George Washington

Bribing voters was common in the colonies as well. Even Washington wasn't above it.

The British king appointed governors of the colonies. Even though each colony had a local government, the governor had authority.

You'll do as I say. King's orders.

Yeah, but the colonial government controlled his salary. So if he wanted to get paid, he had to do what they wanted.

From 1754 to 1763, England fought an expensive war with France.

Guess who didn't get to say if their taxes paid for the war--the colonists (and their horses!).

Shall we tax the colonies to pay for the war? Yea or nay?

Yea.

Worse, British soldiers occupied the colonies. In April 1775, shots rang out between the British and the colonists. The Revolutionary War (1775-1783) began.

We colonists were NOT happy about that.

The colonies needed a government while at war. Members of each colony's government voted on who to send to the Continental Congress.

Patrick Henry for Congress. Yea or nay?

Yea.

At first, the colonies just wanted representation in Parliament. But as the war went on, more colonists wanted freedom from British rule. On July 2, 1776, Congress declared independence from Britain.

July 2 will be celebrated for centuries to come.

Boy was he wrong! We actually celebrate on July 4. That's when the Declaration of Independence was approved.

John Adams

Representatives from 12 of the 13 states voted for independence. New York's representatives didn't vote. They weren't sure what their citizens wanted.

CHAPTER TWO: NEW NATION, NEW LAWS

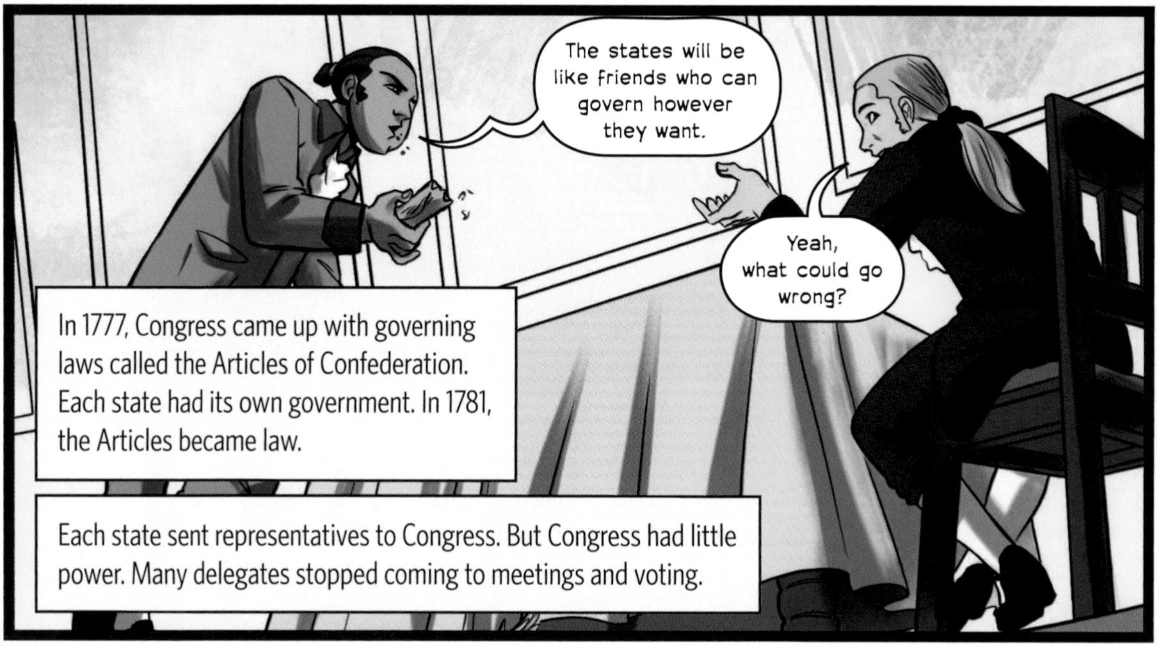
The states will be like friends who can govern however they want.
Yeah, what could go wrong?
In 1777, Congress came up with governing laws called the Articles of Confederation. Each state had its own government. In 1781, the Articles became law.
Each state sent representatives to Congress. But Congress had little power. Many delegates stopped coming to meetings and voting.

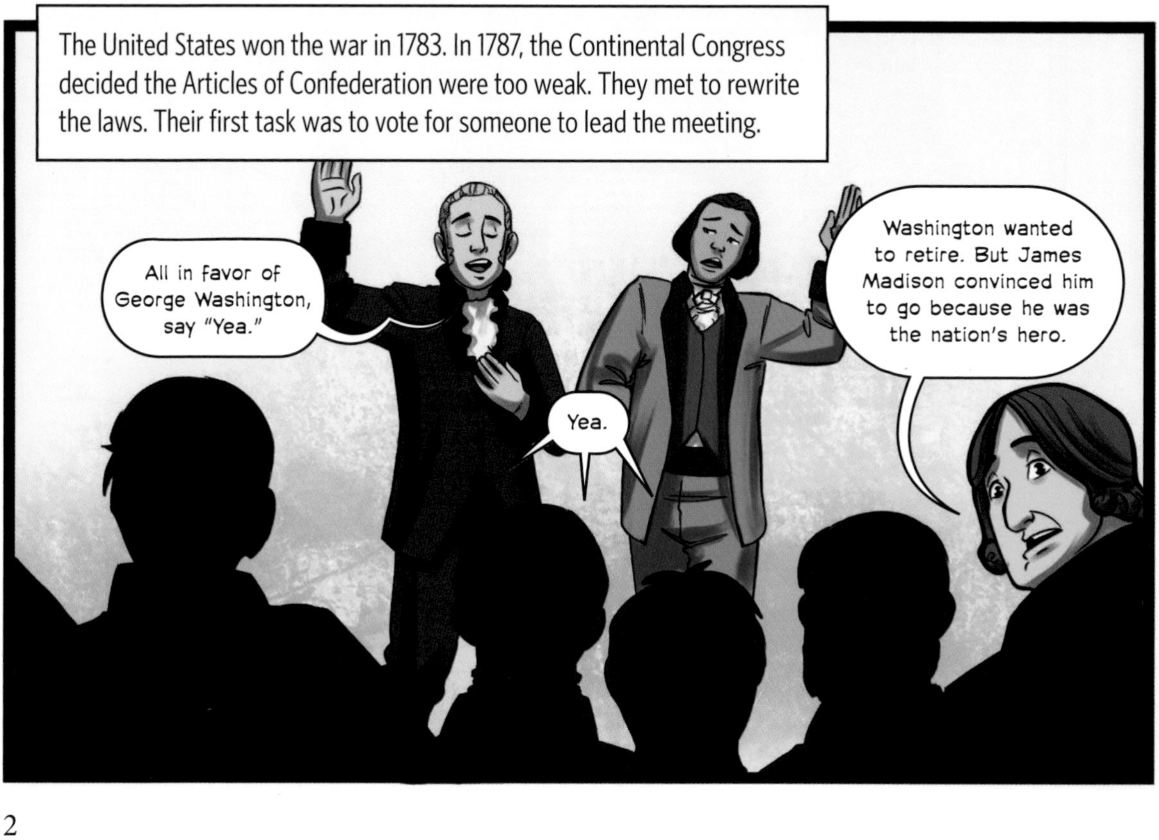
The United States won the war in 1783. In 1787, the Continental Congress decided the Articles of Confederation were too weak. They met to rewrite the laws. Their first task was to vote for someone to lead the meeting.
All in favor of George Washington, say "Yea."
Yea.
Washington wanted to retire. But James Madison convinced him to go because he was the nation's hero.

Congress created a new Constitution. The new U.S. government would have three branches—Legislative, Executive, and Judicial. The Legislative branch had a Senate and a House of Representatives. Each state had two senators. The number of representatives was based on the state's population.

Citizens of each state would vote for their senators and representatives.

When should elections be held?

Let the states decide.

Who should choose the president?

The people, of course.

But there's so many people.

And then the president would favor bigger states over small ones.

Each state decided when to hold state and local elections and how and where the citizens should vote.

That didn't work well for North Carolina and Rhode Island. Their elections were so late, they didn't have any representatives in the first session of Congress in 1789.

The Continental Congress decided on a process, which became known as the Electoral College.

Citizens vote their choice for president.

Officials in that state count the votes to see who got the most.

Each state gets electors based on the number of people it has in Congress. The election winner in each state receives all its electors' votes.

That's not quite true. Today, two states—Nebraska and Maine—split their vote. They give two votes to the statewide winner. The other votes go to the popular winner in specific areas.

The winner needs at least 270 electoral votes.

CHAPTER THREE

SERIOUSLY, WHY CAN'T WE VOTE?

In early America, only white male landowners over the age of 21 could vote.

Stop.

In many states you had to be a Protestant Christian. If you were Catholic, any other religion, or not religious, forget it. So far, all of America's presidents have had a Christian background.

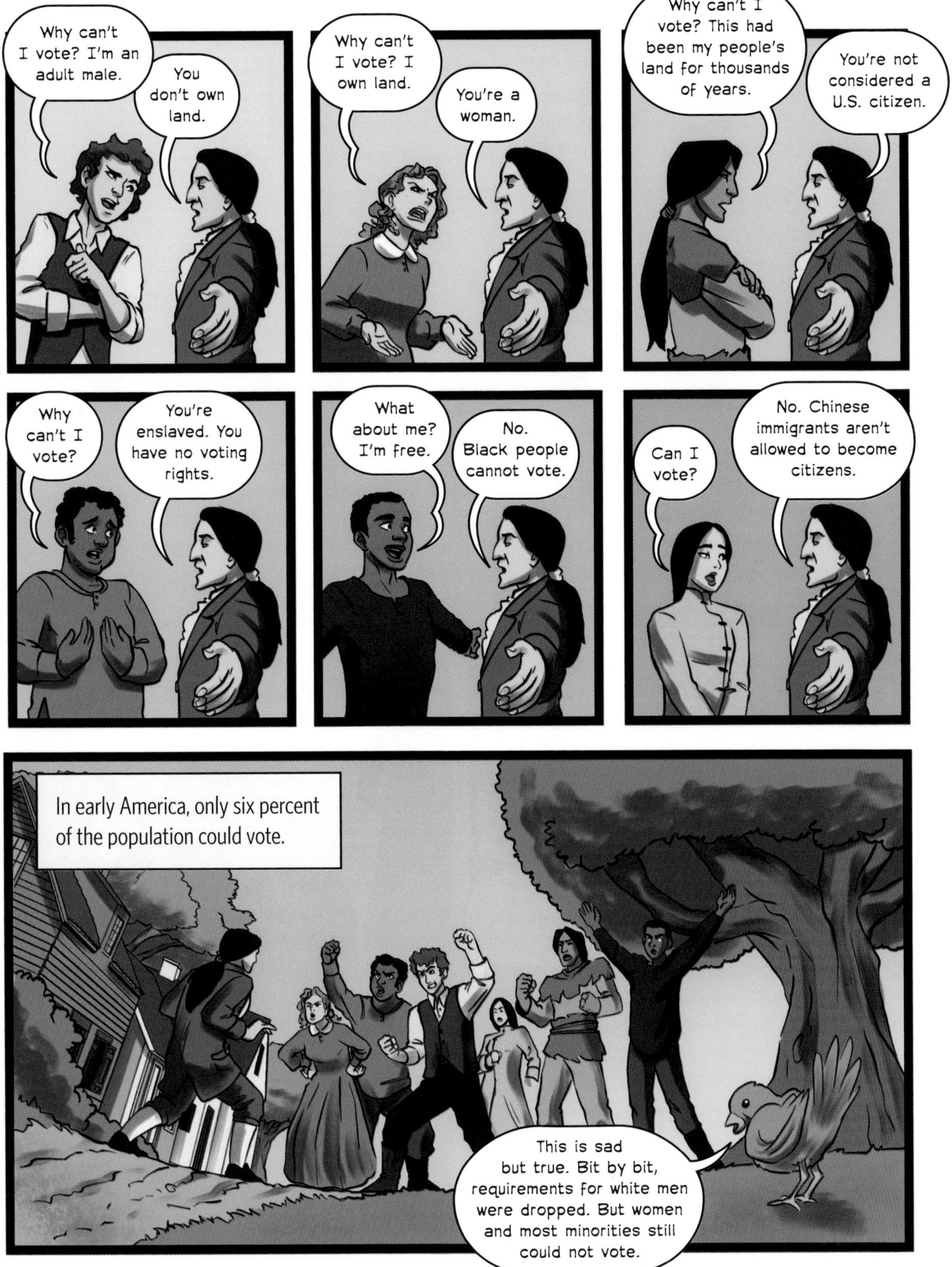
Why can't I vote? I'm an adult male.
You don't own land.
Why can't I vote? I own land.
You're a woman.
Why can't I vote? This had been my people's land for thousands of years.
You're not considered a U.S. citizen.
Why can't I vote?
You're enslaved. You have no voting rights.
What about me? I'm free.
No. Black people cannot vote.
Can I vote?
No. Chinese immigrants aren't allowed to become citizens.
In early America, only six percent of the population could vote.
This is sad but true. Bit by bit, requirements for white men were dropped. But women and most minorities still could not vote.

In 1860, Abraham Lincoln was elected president. Southern states feared he would end slavery, so they formed the Confederate States of America. The Civil War (1861–1865) broke out in April 1861 and lasted four years.

The Union won the war. Less than a year later, enslavement was outlawed in the U.S.

In a public speech on April 11, 1865, Lincoln mentioned Black voting rights. It upset many Southerners, especially John Wilkes Booth.

Lincoln

He wants votes for Black men.

Booth

Booth had been planning to kidnap Lincoln. The speech drove him to anger. He killed Lincoln three days later.

We must have the right to vote.

Douglass

Lincoln's death didn't stop the fight for voting rights for Black men. Frederick Douglass was a formerly enslaved man who spoke for equal voting rights.

Supporters pushed for the Fifteenth Amendment to the Constitution. It became law in 1870. It stated that the right to vote could not be denied because of a person's race. By 1877, about 2,000 Black men were elected to political office. Sixteen served in Congress.

FACT!

Before the Fifteenth Amendment, only Maryland, Massachusetts, New York, North Carolina, Pennsylvania, and Vermont allowed Black men to vote.

Many white people in the South were angry about the progress Black people were making. They didn't want Black men voting. So, they made rules that got around the Fifteenth Amendment. These were called "Black Codes."

You have to pay to vote.

But that's two weeks' pay.

Vote
$ 1.50

Many southern states had poll fees. Black people weren't paid as much as white people and couldn't afford the fees. Some white voters got angry at the tax too. So states enacted "grandfather clauses." The clauses stated that if you or your ancestors could vote before the Civil War, you didn't have to pay.

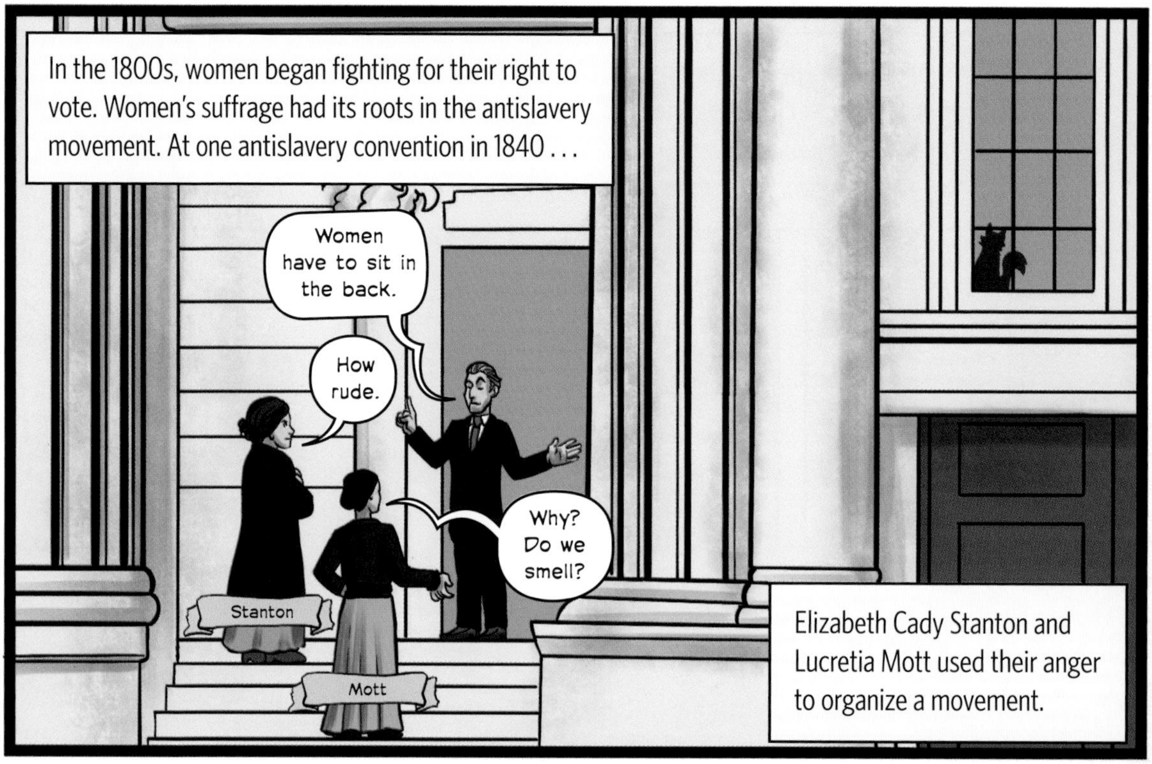
In the 1800s, women began fighting for their right to vote. Women's suffrage had its roots in the antislavery movement. At one antislavery convention in 1840 . . .
Women have to sit in the back.
How rude.
Why? Do we smell?
Stanton
Mott
Elizabeth Cady Stanton and Lucretia Mott used their anger to organize a movement.

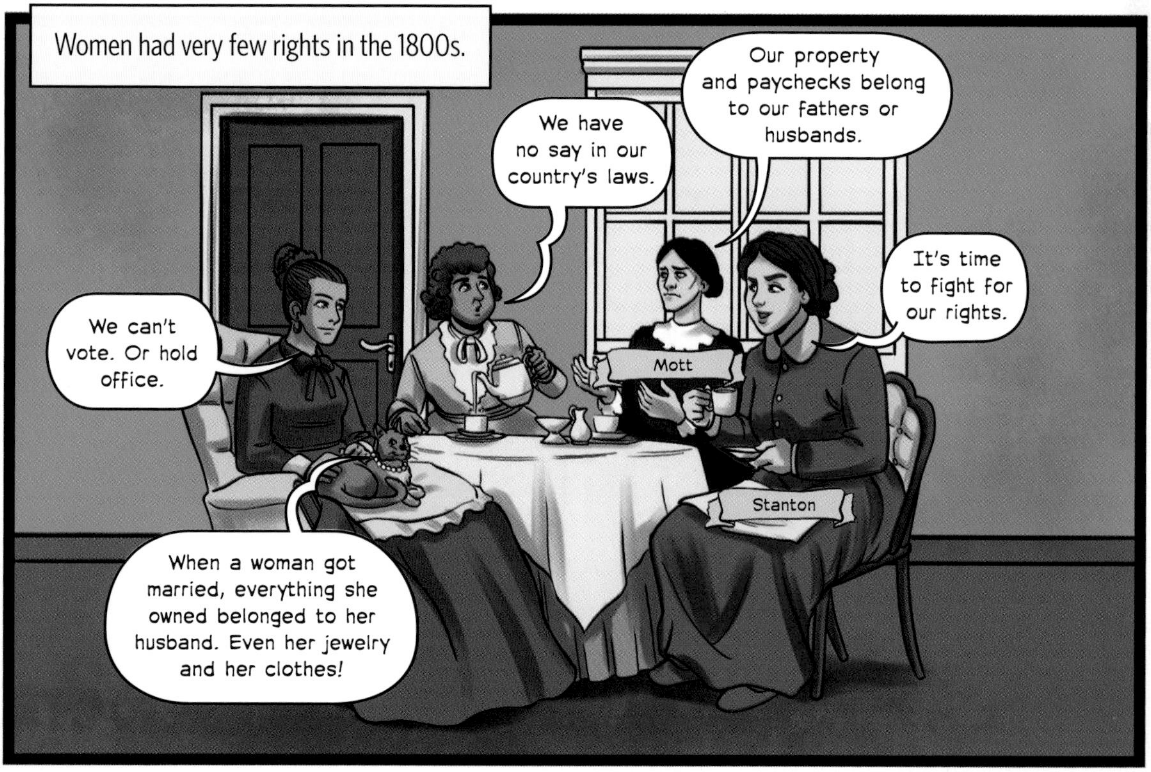
Women had very few rights in the 1800s.
We can't vote. Or hold office.
We have no say in our country's laws.
Our property and paychecks belong to our fathers or husbands.
It's time to fight for our rights.
Mott
Stanton
When a woman got married, everything she owned belonged to her husband. Even her jewelry and her clothes!

In 1848, Stanton and Mott organized a gathering for women's rights in Seneca Falls, New York.

We declare our right . . . to be represented in the government.

Stanton

In the early 1850s, Susan B. Anthony helped lead the women's suffrage movement. She led marches and held rallies.

We will suffer for suffrage.

VOTES FOR WOMEN!

VOTES FOR WOMEN!

VOTES FOR WOMEN!

Anthony

Suffragists definitely suffered. But the word "suffrage" actually comes from a Latin word meaning "the right or privilege to vote."

The people who opposed women voting had odd arguments. "You do not need a ballot to clean out your sink spout," and "Women will need to leave the husband alone with the children in order to go vote."

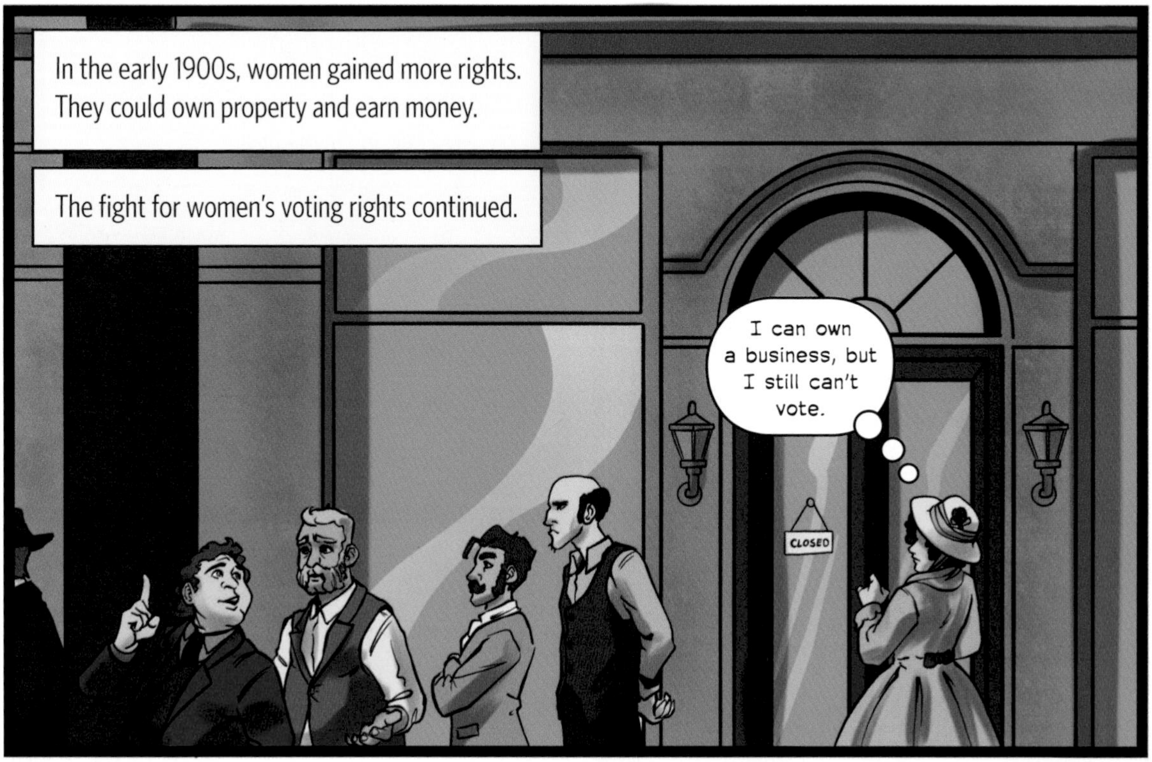
In the early 1900s, women gained more rights. They could own property and earn money.
The fight for women's voting rights continued.
CLOSED
I can own a business, but I still can't vote.

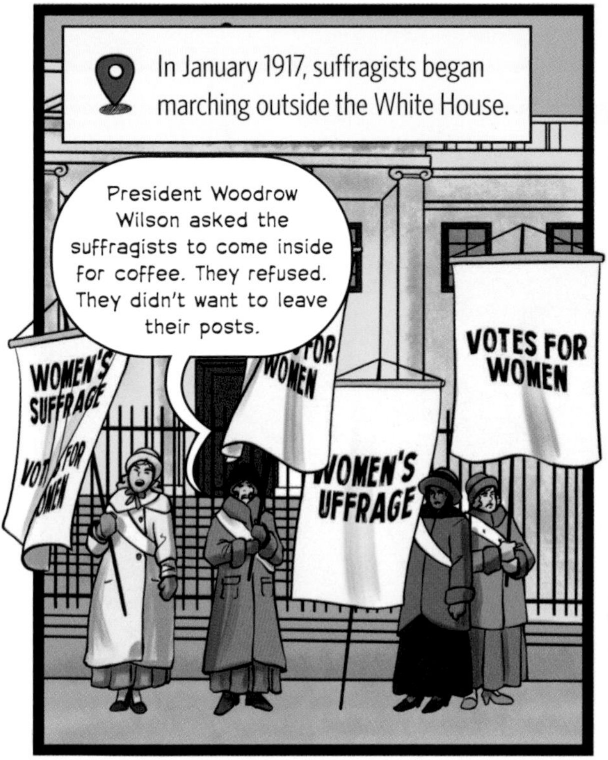
In January 1917, suffragists began marching outside the White House.
President Woodrow Wilson asked the suffragists to come inside for coffee. They refused. They didn't want to leave their posts.
WOMEN'S SUFFRAGE
VOTES FOR WOMEN

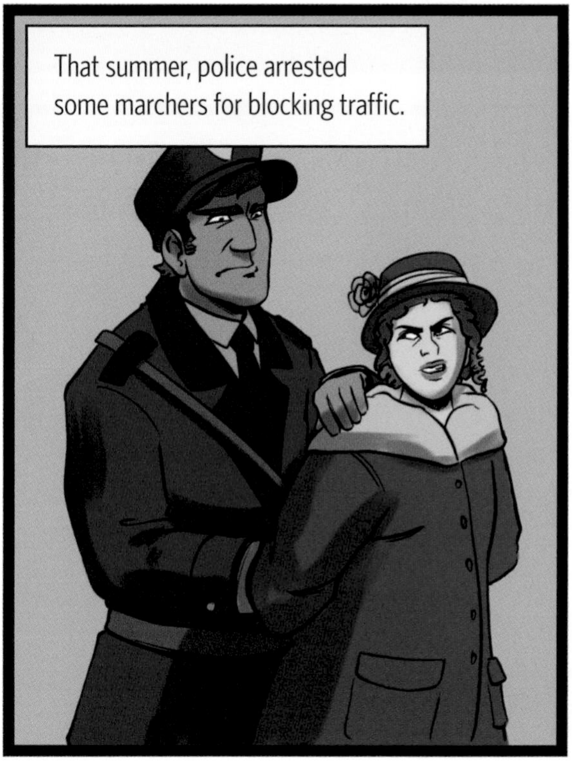
That summer, police arrested some marchers for blocking traffic.

Some of the women went on hunger strikes.

I will not eat until I can vote.

Prison doctors even tried to force-feed them. Didn't they know these brave women wouldn't give up?

Many lawmakers thought women's right to vote should be for states to decide.

In 1869, Wyoming became the first state to allow women to vote. By 1920, fifteen states had given voting rights to women.

FACT!

In 1872, Victoria Woodhull became the first woman to run for president.

But suffragists wanted voting to be nationwide. They pushed for an amendment to the Constitution.

In 1920, the Nineteenth Amendment became law. It stated that the right to vote should not be denied based on sex. Women of color still faced more barriers to voting than white people, though.

CHAPTER FOUR: THE FIGHT FOR VOTING CONTINUES

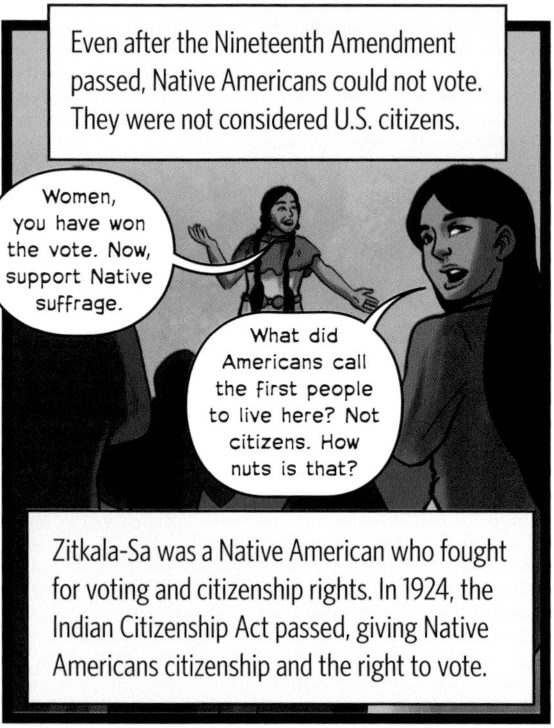
Even after the Nineteenth Amendment passed, Native Americans could not vote. They were not considered U.S. citizens.
Women, you have won the vote. Now, support Native suffrage.
What did Americans call the first people to live here? Not citizens. How nuts is that?
Zitkala-Sa was a Native American who fought for voting and citizenship rights. In 1924, the Indian Citizenship Act passed, giving Native Americans citizenship and the right to vote.

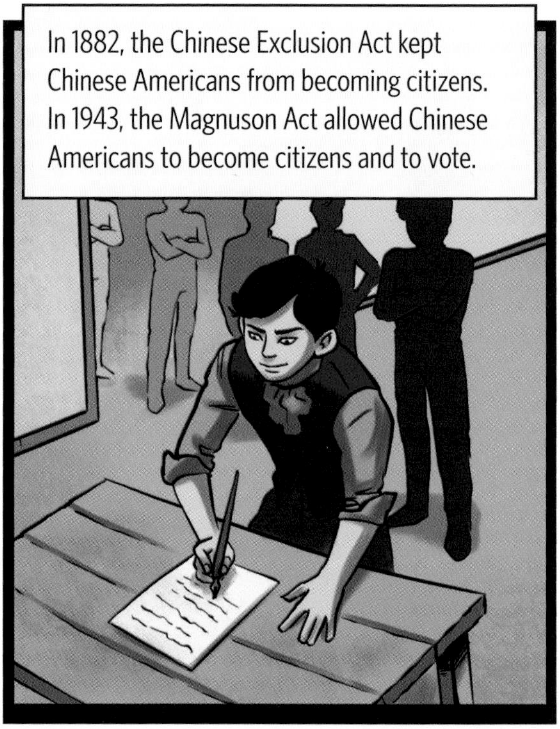
In 1882, the Chinese Exclusion Act kept Chinese Americans from becoming citizens. In 1943, the Magnuson Act allowed Chinese Americans to become citizens and to vote.

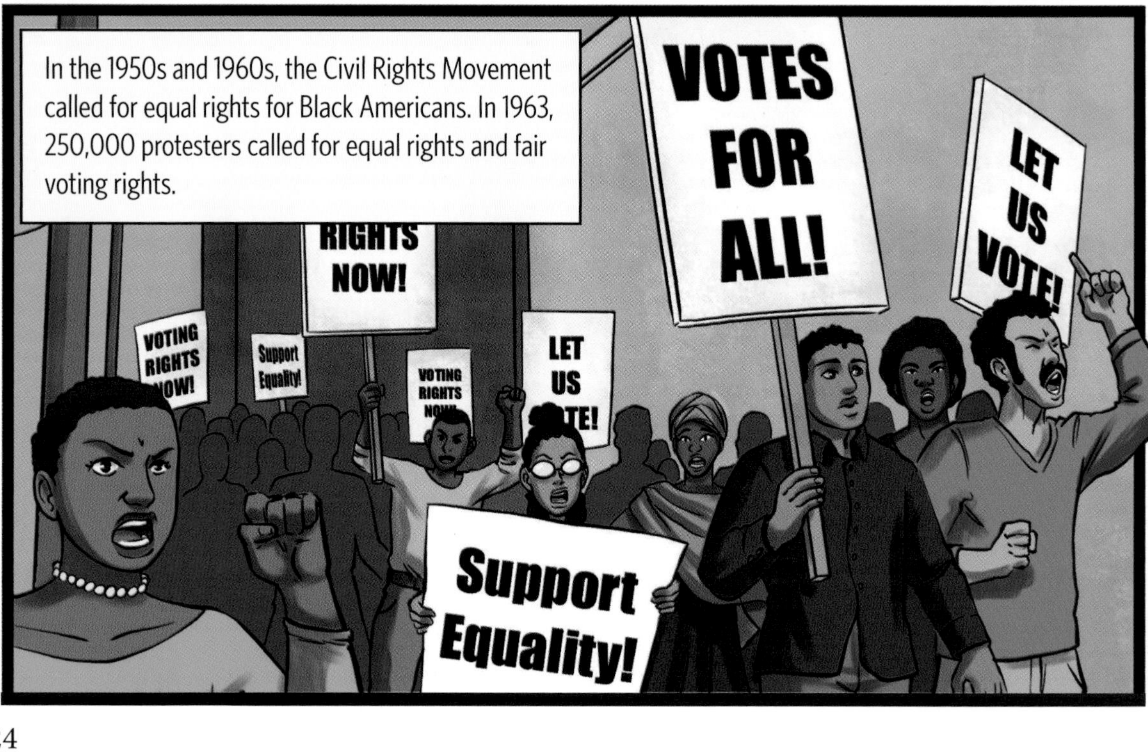
In the 1950s and 1960s, the Civil Rights Movement called for equal rights for Black Americans. In 1963, 250,000 protesters called for equal rights and fair voting rights.
VOTES FOR ALL!
LET US VOTE!
RIGHTS NOW!
Support Equality!
LET US
Support Equality!

In 1964, the Twenty-fourth Amendment to the Constitution made poll taxes illegal. President Lyndon B. Johnson supported it.

THE SELMA CAMPAIGN

In 1965, only two percent of the Black population in Selma, Alabama, was registered to vote. Some Black people who tried to register had to take difficult tests or were turned away. Others were beaten or even killed. Dr. Martin Luther King Jr. organized a voter registration campaign in Selma. He led marches to highlight the importance of equal voting rights. On March 7, police attacked marchers on a bridge. On March 21, protesters marched 54 miles from Selma to Montgomery. More than 25,000 people joined them. The march helped raise awareness of the issues Black voters faced.

The Voting Rights Act of 1965 aimed to prevent any barriers to voting at the state and local levels.

Today, voters turn out for local, state, and national elections. They vote for government leaders and decide some state or local laws.

NO

YES

Americans turn out the most for presidential elections every four years. Presidential campaigns are often exciting and competitive. In the 2000 presidential race, George W. Bush and Al Gore were neck and neck.

Bush

Gore

I bet Gore won.

No, I'm sure Bush won.

The race is too close to call.

FACT! In five presidential elections, candidates became president without winning the popular vote.

In Florida, the race was really close. They recounted the votes. Some ballots were very difficult to determine because of hanging chads.

Chad. Get down.

No, not that Chad.

There was mass chad confusion! Some ballots in Florida used a hole-punch method. Some incomplete hole punches were referred to as hanging chads. It was hard to tell who the voter meant to choose.

George W. Bush ended up narrowly winning Florida. He won the presidency with 271-266 Electoral College votes. But Al Gore won the popular vote by 500,000 votes.

How you vote depends on where you live. Some states use paper ballots that are scanned by an electronic reader. Others use voting machines. Some states use mail-in ballots.

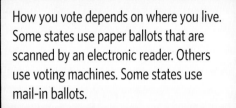

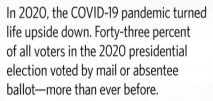

In 2020, the COVID-19 pandemic turned life upside down. Forty-three percent of all voters in the 2020 presidential election voted by mail or absentee ballot—more than ever before.

In 1950, South Carolina began requiring voters to show identification (ID) to vote. More states followed. As of 2023, thirty-six states required some form of ID to vote.

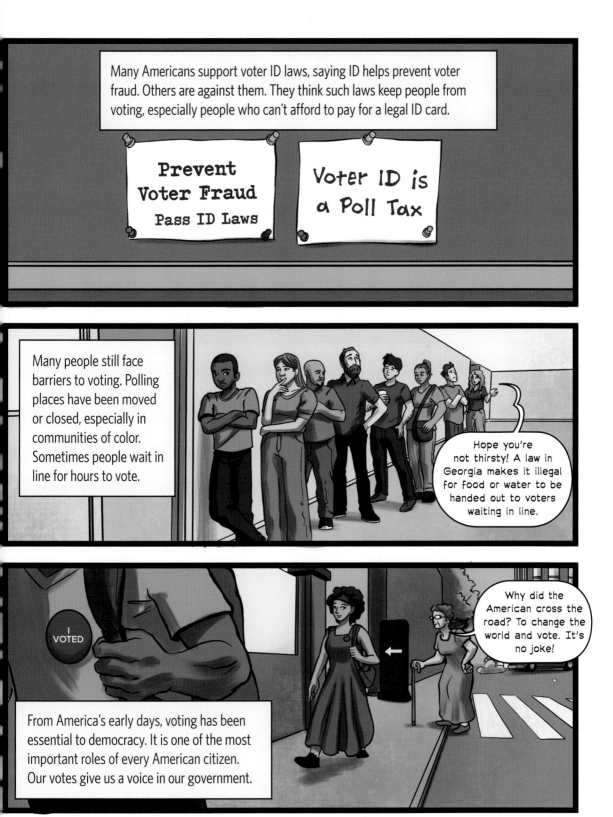

Many Americans support voter ID laws, saying ID helps prevent voter fraud. Others are against them. They think such laws keep people from voting, especially people who can't afford to pay for a legal ID card.

Prevent Voter Fraud
Pass ID Laws

Voter ID is a Poll Tax

Many people still face barriers to voting. Polling places have been moved or closed, especially in communities of color. Sometimes people wait in line for hours to vote.

Hope you're not thirsty! A law in Georgia makes it illegal for food or water to be handed out to voters waiting in line.

I VOTED

Why did the American cross the road? To change the world and vote. It's no joke!

From America's early days, voting has been essential to democracy. It is one of the most important roles of every American citizen. Our votes give us a voice in our government.

GLOSSARY

amendment (uh-MEND-muhnt)—a formal change made to a law or legal document, such as the U.S. Constitution

ancestor (AN-ses-tuhr)—a member of a person's family who lived a long time ago

authority (uh-THAW-ruh-tee)—power or command

ballot (BAL-uht)—a paper or means to cast a vote

citizen (SI-tuh-zuhn)—a member of a country or state who has the right to live there

colony (KAH-luh-nee)—an area that has been settled by people from another country; a colony is ruled by another country

democracy (di-MAH-kruh-see)—a form of government in which the people elect their leaders

protester (PROH-tess-tuhr)—a person who speaks out about something strongly and publicly

READ MORE

Howard, Sherry. *Presidential Elections.* Huntington Beach, CA: Teacher Created Materials, 2022.

Humphrey, Natalie. *Women's Suffrage.* New York: Enslow Publishing, 2023.

Tyner, Artika R. *Black Voter Suppression: The Fight for the Right to Vote.* Minneapolis: Lerner Publishing, 2021.

INTERNET SITES

Britannica Kids: Elections
kids.britannica.com/students/article/elections/274143

Ducksters: United States Government: How Voting Works
ducksters.com/history/us_government_voting.php

History for Kids: Voting Rights Act of 1965 Facts for Kids
historyforkids.org/voting-rights-act-of-1965/

National Geographic Kids: The Women's Suffrage Movement
kids.nationalgeographic.com/history/article/womens-suffrage-movement

ABOUT THE AUTHOR

Jessica Gunderson grew up in the small town of Washburn, North Dakota. She has a bachelor's degree from the University of North Dakota and an MFA in Creative Writing from Minnesota State University, Mankato. She has written more than one hundred books for young readers. Her book *President Lincoln's Killer and the America He Left Behind* won a 2018 Eureka! Nonfiction Children's Book Silver Award. She currently lives in Madison, Wisconsin.

ABOUT THE ILLUSTRATOR

Luiz Fernando da Silva is an illustrator and comic artist from Santa Catarina, Brazil. As a child, he created his own stories for fun, based on his favorite cartoons and video games. Luiz started his career as an illustrator and designer in 2006. He has been a full-time illustrator for more than 10 years. In his free time, he likes to watch movies and TV, play video games, read, and barbecue.